The Intentional Day Planner

by Julie Singer

Invite miracles into each and every day!

"Your vision will become clear
only when you look into your heart.

Who looks outside dreams,
who looks inside awakens."

– Carl Jung

This magical faery book belongs to:

_JJ_ ♡

If found, with deepest gratitude,
thank you for its safe return.

Thank you to Jessica Joliecoeur for your beautiful artistic talent throughout this book, as well as the graphic design work by Faye Wilson and Greg Sykes.

Thank you to Garry Johnson at Hip & Cool Marketing for helping me to complete this book and a deep heartfelt gratitude to my friends and family who have supported and encouraged me every step along the way.

Thanks,

Julie

My Gift to Myself

I am giving myself the gift of unlimited possibilities,
of presence and inner peace.

I am wise.

I am worthy.

I am giving myself permission to get clear on what my dreams are
and know that I have the power to manifest them.

I am creative.

I am capable.

I am aware of my thoughts and I know that they play
a role in creating my reality.

I am a divinely inspired.

I am divinely guided.

I am remembering my connection to all of life, to nature,
and to the cosmos.

I am the love that creates this Universe.

I am free!

Ready to become a conscious co-creator?

The Intentional Day Planner is a fun and flexible tool that is designed to help you harness the natural energies of the lunar cycle, along with the power of intentions and gratitude, to manifest a life you love.

Congratulations! You have given yourself a wonderful gift and taken the first step in playing a more active role in co-creating your amazing life. The second step is to check out the lunar calendar on the pages that follow, see which new moon you wish to start on and write in the date in the space provided. The third, and most important step, is to tune into your heart and follow where you are being guided.

You are here on purpose and you have important gifts to share with the rest of the world. Remember it isn't about doing more, it is about being in harmony with the spirit of Intention. Trust the flow. You are now on your way to becoming a conscious co-creator.

What is The Intentional Day Planner and how do I use it?

At the beginning of each lunar cycle, there is a place for you to keep a list of your new moon intentions, goals and dreams. The new moon is a time of beginnings. When declaring your intentions for the month ahead you are planting those seeds in a fertile field of energy. Completing this work within 48 hours of the new moon will ensure that you are capturing these natural energies in their most potent form.

"...abundance and joy."

The energies of the new moon shift into the waxing moon, which continues to support you as you build and cultivate your intentions. At the time of the full moon all your intuition, inspiration, creativity and emotions are at their peak waiting for you to channel these energies into manifesting your unique dreams and visions. The waning moon's energies are best suited for completion, tying up loose ends, completing your to do lists and harvesting the fruits of your intentions. With the new moon approaching once again, there is a sense of urgency to get things done, so you are ready to ride the next wave of this natural cycle.

As you progress through the lunar cycle you are able to track the stages of the moon using the icons across the top of the page. Being aware of these energies may help you remember your connection to the cosmos and the heavens. You may also choose to schedule your days in the flow of these energies, adding more ease and grace to your days.

The Intentional Day Planner is infused with joy which permeates the pages, along with magic from the faeries, which dance throughout. Look for places where you can invite your imaginative spirit to come out to play and creatively express what is in your heart. Breathe, be still, open your heart and see what pours forth. Listen. What does your heart have to say? With divine inspiration as your guide, declare what you want to experience and write it down. What do you wish to accomplish? What support do you need to do so? Is your heart being called to action? These daily intentions will help you build on smaller successes to assist you in realizing your greater new moon goals.

Each lunar cycle is 29.5 days, however, because The Intentional Day Planner is designed for 30 days of intentions and gratitude, you may at times notice an extra day at the end of the cycle. If the new moon is here and you still have one day left to write in your planner, skip that day and go to the next new moon section. This will help you stay in synch with the natural energies of the moon and the flow of The Intentional Day Planner.

"...activating the energy of gratitude."

The most important element of The Intentional Day Planner is activating the energy of gratitude. Take time each day to reflect and meditate on what you have to be grateful for. Say "thank you" for all of the amazing gifts in your life. Activating the energy of gratitude is the most important part of co-creation. Remember, each day is an opportunity to begin anew and consciously co-create the life of your dreams!

Lunar Calendar 2015

NEW MOON

20 January 2015 13:14:49	16 July 2015 01:25:33
18 February 2015 23:48:21	14 August 2015 14:54:40
20 March 2015 09:37:18	13 September 2015 06:42:35
18 April 2015 18:57:59	13 October 2015 00:07:02
18 May 2015 04:14:19	11 November 2015 17:48:21
16 June 2015 14:06:27	11 December 2015 10:30:30

FIRST QUARTER

27 January 2015 04:49:30	24 July 2015 04:05:11
25 February 2015 17:15:09	22 August 2015 19:32:16
27 March 2015 07:43:48	21 September 2015 09:00:18
25 April 2015 23:56:25	20 October 2015 20:32:30
25 May 2015 17:20:10	19 November 2015 06:28:33
24 June 2015 11:03:47	18 December 2015 15:15:27

FULL MOON

5 January 2015 04:54:29	2 July 2015 02:20:45
3 February 2015 23:10:13	31 July 2015 10:44:03
5 March 2015 18:06:40	29 August 2015 18:36:17
4 April 2015 12:06:52	28 September 2015 02:51:37
4 May 2015 03:43:23	27 October 2015 12:06:15
2 June 2015 16:20:13	25 November 2015 22:45:18
	25 December 2015 11:12:31

LAST QUARTER

13 January 2015 09:47:44	8 July 2015 20:25:01
12 February 2015 03:51:11	7 August 2015 02:03:50
13 March 2015 17:49:13	5 September 2015 09:55:19
12 April 2015 03:45:38	4 October 2015 21:07:15
11 May 2015 10:37:18	3 November 2015 12:24:59
9 June 2015 15:42:54	3 December 2015 07:41:35

IMPORTANT DATES:

World Peace and Gratitude Day:	*21 September 2015*
Spring Equinox:	*20 March 2015*
Summer Solstice:	*21 June 2015*
Fall Equinox:	*23 September 2015*
Winter Solstice:	*22 December 2015*

Lunar Calendar 2016

NEW MOON

10 January 2016
01:31:38

8 February 2016
14:40:02

9 March 2016
01:55:33

7 April 2016
11:24:47

6 May 2016
19:30:44

5 June 2016
03:00:45

4 July 2016
11:02:10

2 August 2016
20:45:48

1 September 2016
09:04:25

1 October 2016
00:12:45

30 October 2016
17:39:36

29 November 2016
12:19:35

29 December 2016
06:53:00

FIRST QUARTER

16 January 2016
23:27:25

15 February 2016
07:47:34

15 March 2016
17:04:04

14 April 2016
04:00:32

13 May 2016
17:03:26

12 June 2016
08:11:10

12 July 2016
00:53:11

10 August 2016
18:22:12

9 September 2016
11:50:13

9 October 2016
04:34:22

7 November 2016
19:52:27

7 December 2016
09:04:13

FULL MOON

24 January 2016
01:46:55

22 February 2016
18:21:05

23 March 2016
12:02:02

22 April 2016
05:24:54

21 May 2016
21:15:45

20 June 2016
11:03:34

19 July 2016
22:57:51

18 August 2016
09:27:50

16 September 2016
19:06:17

16 October 2016
04:24:18

14 November 2016
13:53:16

14 December 2016
00:06:42

LAST QUARTER

2 January 2016
05:31:36

1 February 2016
03:29:00

1 March 2016
23:12:01

31 March 2016
15:18:11

30 April 2016
03:30:00

29 May 2016
12:13:12

27 June 2016
18:19:46

26 July 2016
23:00:46

25 August 2016
03:42:00

23 September 2016
09:57:21

22 October 2016
19:15:07

21 November 2016
08:34:32

21 December 2016
01:57:01

IMPORTANT DATES:

World Peace and Gratitude Day:	*21 September 2016*
Spring Equinox:	*20 March 2016*
Summer Solstice:	*20 June 2016*
Fall Equinox:	*22 September 2016*
Winter Solstice:	*21 December*

My Inspirational Journey for The Intentional Day Planner by Julie Singer

*A*s a child, I remember the incredible feeling of being out in the garden, amongst the sweet peas, knowing in my heart, with complete certainty, that the faery kingdom is all around us.

The feeling could be described as, excited anticipation, as though anything was possible, it was only up to me to dream and it would be so. I would play in the forest behind our house and I would be constantly reminded of the unseen world just beyond.

The sunlight dancing through the drops of dew, reflecting brilliant rays of light... or was that a faery out of the corner of my eye. I would strain to see, heart open wide and overflowing with joy, for the opportunity to step into a space filled with bliss, wonder and amazement. I could stay there for hours, like a dream you didn't want to wake up from.

Over time, as I got older, I forgot how to find my way back to this magical world. For many years I went to sleep, but I did not dream. I grew up quickly, going through many of the challenges that kids face when their parents divorce. I was also diagnosed with Crohn's disease, a chronic inflammatory bowel condition, just before starting high school.

I underwent many challenges, physically, mentally and emotionally. It became hard to see the beauty and sparkle in life anymore. Most of my adult life was spent in this slumber, the pain so intense, that I often believed that all life had to offer was mistrust and fear.

For over twenty years, I tried almost every drug, diet and natural treatment available. During this time I also began to notice how important my mindset was on my physical wellbeing.

I truly felt my best when I was happy despite the physical challenges I was facing. There were a few treasured days where I was completely in tune with my joy and it was in those times that I was honestly able to forget that I had a chronic illness, even if just for a brief moment.

The Intentional Day Planner was created during some of my most challenging as well as joyful days. During this time I was living in Roberts Creek, on the Sunshine Coast.

I felt closely connected to nature and the unseen world just beyond. I would sit on the veranda, the autumn sun on my face, fueling me with warmth from the inside out. I felt tremendous waves of joy and appreciation as I watched the leaves of the oak and maple trees change color and fall. I felt a similar process going on inside me.

I realized the importance of surrendering to, and being present with, the pain. It was amazing the energy that was freed up when I finally gave up control and stopped trying so hard to "be well." It didn't matter what was happening in my physical body, what mattered was how I would choose to respond. Would I do so with love or with fear?

I set the intention that I was going to learn from this and embrace the life I was being offered, rather than focusing on the limitations and the loss.

I was waking up. I could see the vibrancy of the colors, life came alive for me again and my belief in miracles was restored. I wanted to skip again and share the love I felt inside with everyone. I remembered how to connect with myself, and with nature. I had uncovered the power of intentions and the incredible importance of gratitude.

I was still undergoing many health challenges, they actually intensified during this time, and I eventually underwent surgery in 2012 after exhausting all other options. I had my entire large intestine removed and I now live with an ileostomy.

It took an incredible amount of faith and courage to make that choice but I am so glad I did. I am still uncovering why I have been guided down this path, but I know the gifts I have, and continue to receive, are truly priceless.

The Intentional Day Planner was born out of a heartfelt desire to create a tool that brings joy and playfulness into peoples' experience while also inspiring and empowering them to be more active participants in their lives.

I believe that every single one of us has everything we need within, to co-create the life of our dreams. I intend for my heart to know no limits and for the love to flow, free from fear, regardless of what life presents.

Life is full of ups and downs, joys and sorrows – the question we need to ask ourselves is how wide can we open our hearts to embrace everything that is being offered?

My Gift To You!

Now that you know a little bit of my story and why I'm passionate about passing on tips and resources to help others through challenging times, I'd like to offer you this simple and easy to follow plan for the next 21 days to see the power it can have in your life.

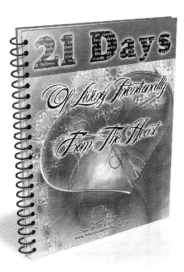

21 Days of Living Intentionally from the Heart

Here is a plan to help you get started shifting your life so you can live each day from a more heart centered and intentional place. Why 21 days, you may ask, well that is how long it takes to change a habit.

My intention is to provide you with a simple tool that you can follow for 21 days that will inspire and empower you to live more fully from this heart centered place.

You can get this FREE digital download simply by going to the following website address and click the "Claim Now" button on the page.

Enter the following address into your internet browser for immediate access. www.IntentionalDayPlanner.com/21days

This 21 day guide will give you step by step directions to establish the habit of living intentionally from the heart.

You'll get:
7 days of Contemplations to impact your day
7 days of Intentions to clarify your direction
7 days of Actions to positively affect your life

This free ebook is a great supplement to your Intentional Day Planner and will help to stimulate ideas for what to write in your planner for the first 21 days.

Thank you for purchasing your Intention Day Planner, I truly hope that it serves you and continues to deliver more joy, happiness, freedom and success as you use it.

Heartfully,

Julie

Set your New Moon intentions:

Set your New Moon intentions:

New Moon   On this day

My intentions are

I am grateful for

On this day

My intentions are

I am grateful for

On this day

My intentions are

I am grateful for

On this day _____

My intentions are

_____

_____

_____

_____

_____

_____

_____

_____

_____

I am grateful for

_____

_____

_____

_____

_____

_____

_____

_____

On this day _____

My intentions are _____

_____

_____

_____

_____

_____

_____

_____

_____

_____

_____

I am grateful for _____

_____

_____

_____

_____

_____

_____

_____

_____

_____

On this day _____

My intentions are _____

I am grateful for _____

On this day _____

My intentions are _____

_____
_____
_____
_____
_____
_____
_____
_____
_____
_____

I am grateful for _____

_____
_____
_____
_____
_____
_____
_____
_____
_____
_____

On this day

My intentions are

I am grateful for

On this day

My intentions are

I am grateful for

On this day _____

My intentions are _____

_____

_____

_____

_____

_____

_____

_____

_____

_____

I am grateful for _____

_____

_____

_____

_____

_____

_____

_____

_____

On this day

My intentions are

I am grateful for

On this day _____

My intentions are _____

I am grateful for _____

On this day

My intentions are

I am grateful for

On this day

My intentions are

I am grateful for

On this day _____

My intentions are _____

I am grateful for _____

Full Moon   On this day _____

My intentions are _____
_____
_____
_____
_____
_____
_____
_____
_____
_____
_____

I am grateful for _____
_____
_____
_____
_____
_____
_____
_____
_____

On this day _____

My intentions are _____

I am grateful for _____

On this day

My intentions are

I am grateful for

On this day

My intentions are

I am grateful for

On this day

_____

My intentions are

I am grateful for

On this day _____

My intentions are _____
_____
_____
_____
_____
_____
_____
_____
_____
_____
_____

I am grateful for _____
_____
_____
_____
_____
_____
_____
_____
_____
_____
_____
_____

On this day _____

My intentions are _____

I am grateful for _____

On this day

My intentions are

I am grateful for

On this day _____

My intentions are _____

I am grateful for _____

On this day _____

My intentions are _____

I am grateful for _____

On this day

My intentions are

I am grateful for

On this day

My intentions are

I am grateful for

On this day _____

My intentions are _____

_____

_____

_____

_____

_____

_____

_____

_____

_____

I am grateful for _____

_____

_____

_____

_____

_____

_____

_____

On this day

My intentions are

I am grateful for

On this day _____

My intentions are _____

I am grateful for _____

Write at least ten things you love about yourself:
(Keep going until you fill the entire page)

Set your New Moon intentions:

Set your New Moon intentions:

New Moon   On this day _____

My intentions are _____

_____

_____

_____

_____

_____

_____

_____

_____

I am grateful for _____

_____

_____

_____

_____

_____

_____

_____

_____

On this day _____

My intentions are _____

I am grateful for _____

On this day

My intentions are

I am grateful for

On this day

My intentions are

I am grateful for

On this day _____

My intentions are _____

_____

_____

_____

_____

_____

_____

_____

_____

I am grateful for _____

_____

_____

_____

_____

_____

_____

_____

On this day _____

My intentions are _____

I am grateful for _____

On this day

My intentions are

I am grateful for

On this day _____

My intentions are _____

_____
_____
_____
_____
_____
_____
_____
_____

I am grateful for _____

_____
_____
_____
_____
_____
_____
_____
_____
_____
_____

On this day _____

My intentions are _____

_____

_____

_____

_____

_____

_____

_____

_____

_____

I am grateful for _____

_____

_____

_____

_____

_____

_____

_____

_____

On this day

My intentions are

I am grateful for

On this day _____

My intentions are _____

_____

_____

_____

_____

_____

_____

_____

_____

I am grateful for _____

_____

_____

_____

_____

_____

_____

_____

On this day _____

My intentions are _____

_____
_____
_____
_____
_____
_____
_____
_____
_____

I am grateful for _____

_____
_____
_____
_____
_____
_____
_____
_____
_____
_____

On this day

My intentions are

I am grateful for

On this day

My intentions are

I am grateful for

On this day

My intentions are

I am grateful for

Full Moon

On this day

_____

My intentions are

_____

_____

_____

_____

_____

_____

_____

_____

_____

_____

I am grateful for

_____

_____

_____

_____

_____

_____

_____

_____

_____

_____

On this day _____

My intentions are _____

_____

_____

_____

_____

_____

_____

_____

_____

I am grateful for _____

_____

_____

_____

_____

_____

_____

_____

On this day _____

My intentions are _____

I am grateful for _____

On this day _____

My intentions are _____

_____
_____
_____
_____
_____
_____
_____
_____
_____
_____

I am grateful for _____

_____
_____
_____
_____
_____
_____
_____

On this day _____

My intentions are _____

_____

_____

_____

_____

_____

_____

_____

_____

I am grateful for _____

_____

_____

_____

_____

_____

_____

_____

_____

_____

On this day

My intentions are

I am grateful for

On this day

My intentions are

I am grateful for

On this day _____

My intentions are _____

_____

_____

_____

_____

_____

_____

_____

_____

_____

_____

_____

I am grateful for _____

_____

_____

_____

_____

_____

_____

_____

On this day

My intentions are

I am grateful for

On this day _____

My intentions are _____

_____
_____
_____
_____
_____
_____
_____
_____
_____

I am grateful for _____

_____
_____
_____
_____
_____
_____
_____

On this day _____

My intentions are _____

_____

_____

_____

_____

_____

_____

_____

_____

I am grateful for _____

_____

_____

_____

_____

_____

_____

_____

_____

_____

_____

On this day _____

My intentions are _____

I am grateful for

On this day

My intentions are

I am grateful for

On this day _____

My intentions are _____

_____

_____

_____

_____

_____

_____

_____

_____

I am grateful for _____

_____

_____

_____

_____

_____

_____

_____

_____

On this day _____

My intentions are _____

_____

_____

_____

_____

_____

_____

_____

_____

_____

I am grateful for _____

_____

_____

_____

_____

_____

_____

_____

_____

_____

_____

What fuels your creative spirit? Tell me 10 ways you could invite more creativity into your life.

Set your New Moon intentions:

Set your New Moon intentions:

New Moon

On this day _____

My intentions are _____

_____
_____
_____
_____
_____
_____
_____
_____
_____
_____

I am grateful for _____

_____
_____
_____
_____
_____
_____
_____
_____
_____

On this day

My intentions are

I am grateful for

On this day ....

My intentions are ....

I am grateful for ....

On this day

My intentions are

I am grateful for

On this day _____

My intentions are _____

_____
_____
_____
_____
_____
_____
_____
_____
_____
_____

I am grateful for _____

_____
_____
_____
_____
_____
_____
_____
_____
_____
_____
_____

On this day

My intentions are

I am grateful for

On this day ....

My intentions are ....

....

....

....

....

....

....

....

....

....

I am grateful for ....

....

....

....

....

....

....

....

....

....

On this day

My intentions are

I am grateful for

On this day

My intentions are

I am grateful for

On this day _____

My intentions are _____

I am grateful for _____

On this day _____

My intentions are _____

I am grateful for _____

On this day

My intentions are

I am grateful for

On this day _____

My intentions are _____

_____
_____
_____
_____
_____
_____
_____
_____
_____
_____

I am grateful for _____

_____
_____
_____
_____
_____
_____
_____
_____
_____

On this day

My intentions are

I am grateful for

On this day _____

My intentions are _____

I am grateful for _____

Full Moon

On this day _____

My intentions are _____

_____

_____

_____

_____

_____

_____

_____

_____

I am grateful for _____

_____

_____

_____

_____

_____

_____

_____

_____

_____

_____

On this day _____

My intentions are _____

_____

_____

_____

_____

_____

_____

_____

_____

I am grateful for _____

_____

_____

_____

_____

_____

_____

_____

_____

_____

On this day

My intentions are

I am grateful for

On this day

My intentions are

I am grateful for

On this day

My intentions are

I am grateful for

On this day

My intentions are

I am grateful for

On this day

My intentions are

I am grateful for

On this day

My intentions are

I am grateful for

www.IntentionalDayPlanner.com

On this day

My intentions are

I am grateful for

On this day

My intentions are

I am grateful for

On this day

My intentions are

I am grateful for

On this day

My intentions are

I am grateful for

www.IntentionalDayPlanner.com

On this day

My intentions are

I am grateful for

On this day ....

My intentions are ....

_____
_____
_____
_____
_____
_____
_____
_____

I am grateful for ....

_____
_____
_____
_____
_____
_____
_____
_____
_____
_____

On this day _____

My intentions are _____

_____

_____

_____

_____

_____

_____

_____

_____

_____

I am grateful for _____

_____

_____

_____

_____

_____

_____

_____

_____

_____

Visualize and describe your perfect day:

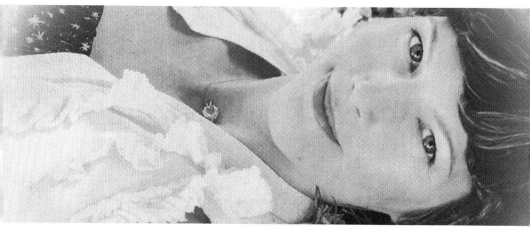

A Chance To Explore
Your Greatest Adventure
With Julie Singer

Vancouver, BC, Canada
From the desk of Julie Singer

Dear friend,

I sincerely hope you are enjoying your Intentional Day Planner. I believe that very few things will make as big of a positive impact on your day to day living as the practice of consciously choosing who you want to be and how you want to show up in life.

Congratulations for making it this far into your planner!

How would you like to explore what your "Greatest Adventure" could be? That's right, even if you are having the time of your life right now, there IS something even better out there for you.

I invite a small group of individuals on a monthly basis to take that journey and look beyond the horizon for what life has in store for you.

There is limited space per month so please visit the web link below and enter your contact information to reserve your spot.
www.IntentionalDayPlanner.com/greatestadventure

Don't worry, if you don't get invinted this month, you are able to enter your name every month for your chance. *(only ONE entry per month will be registered and then the slots are reset on the 1st)*

For approximately 1 hour you will get the chance to work with Julie on:

- Making a clear assessment of how satisfied you are in all areas of your life.
- Targeting the weakest areas and create plans to inject success, joy and celebration.
- Brainstorming for solutions to make your life achievements simple, fun and lasting.
- Taking an active role in creating the life of your dreams.
- Building a community of supportive friends who will inspire, motivate and share stories of success.
- Plus so much more...

>>>> Web Link >>>>
www.IntentionalDayPlanner/greatestadventure

Set your New Moon intentions:

Set your New Moon intentions:

On this day _____

My intentions are _____

I am grateful for _____

On this day _____

My intentions are _____

_____

_____

_____

_____

_____

_____

_____

_____

_____

I am grateful for _____

_____

_____

_____

_____

_____

_____

_____

_____

_____

On this day _____

My intentions are _____

I am grateful for _____

On this day _____

My intentions are _____

_____

_____

_____

_____

_____

_____

_____

_____

_____

I am grateful for _____

_____

_____

_____

_____

_____

_____

_____

_____

_____

_____

_____

On this day _____

My intentions are _____

_____

_____

_____

_____

_____

_____

_____

_____

I am grateful for _____

_____

_____

_____

_____

_____

_____

_____

_____

On this day

My intentions are

I am grateful for

On this day

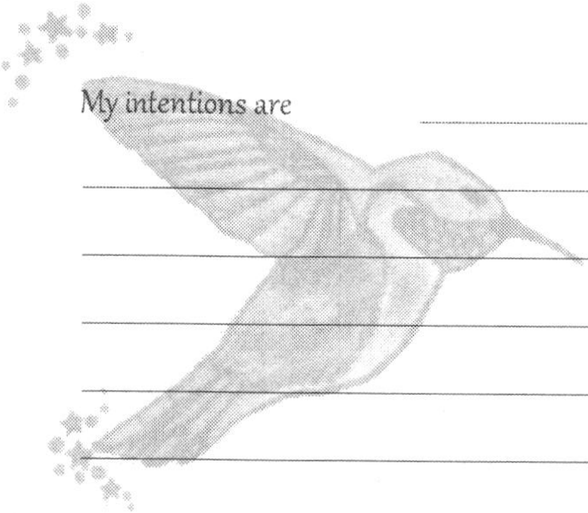

My intentions are

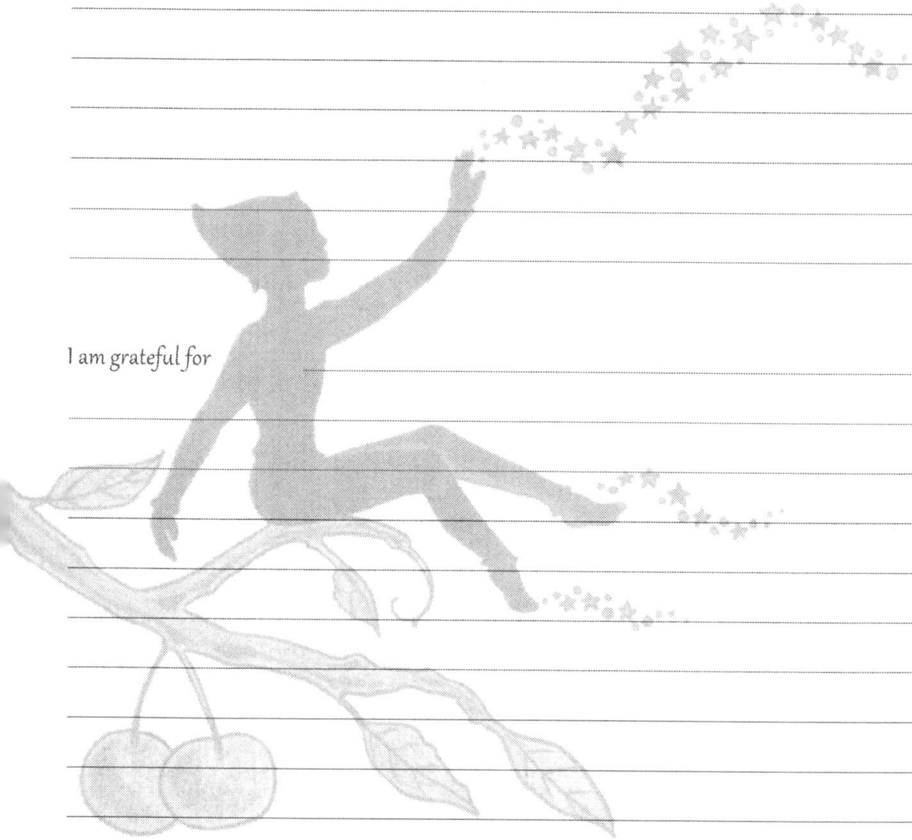

I am grateful for

On this day _____

My intentions are _____

_____
_____
_____
_____
_____
_____
_____
_____
_____

I am grateful for _____

_____
_____
_____
_____
_____
_____
_____
_____
_____
_____
_____

On this day _____

My intentions are _____

_____

_____

_____

_____

_____

_____

_____

I am grateful for _____

_____

_____

_____

_____

_____

_____

_____

On this day _____

My intentions are _____

_____
_____
_____
_____
_____
_____
_____
_____
_____
_____

I am grateful for _____

_____
_____
_____
_____
_____
_____
_____
_____
_____
_____
_____

On this day _____

My intentions are
_____
_____
_____
_____
_____
_____
_____
_____

I am grateful for
_____
_____
_____
_____
_____
_____
_____
_____
_____
_____

On this day

My intentions are

I am grateful for

On this day _____

My intentions are _____

_____

_____

_____

_____

_____

_____

_____

_____

I am grateful for _____

_____

_____

_____

_____

_____

_____

_____

On this day _____

My intentions are _____

_____
_____
_____
_____
_____
_____
_____
_____
_____
_____
_____

I am grateful for _____

_____
_____
_____
_____
_____
_____
_____
_____
_____
_____
_____
_____
_____

On this day _____

My intentions are _____
_____
_____
_____
_____
_____
_____
_____
_____

I am grateful for _____
_____
_____
_____
_____
_____
_____
_____
_____

Full Moon

On this day

My intentions are

I am grateful for

On this day

My intentions are

I am grateful for

On this day

My intentions are

I am grateful for

On this day

My intentions are

I am grateful for

On this day _____

My intentions are _____

I am grateful for _____

On this day

My intentions are

I am grateful for

On this day _____

My intentions are _____

I am grateful for _____

On this day _____

My intentions are _____

_____

_____

_____

_____

_____

_____

_____

I am grateful for _____

_____

_____

_____

_____

_____

_____

_____

_____

On this day

My intentions are

I am grateful for

On this day _____

My intentions are _____

_____

_____

_____

_____

_____

_____

_____

_____

I am grateful for _____

_____

_____

_____

_____

_____

_____

_____

_____

On this day _____

My intentions are _____

_____

_____

_____

_____

_____

_____

_____

_____

_____

I am grateful for _____

_____

_____

_____

_____

_____

_____

_____

_____

_____

_____

On this day

My intentions are

I am grateful for

On this day

My intentions are

I am grateful for

On this day _____

My intentions are _____

I am grateful for

On this day _____

My intentions are _____

_____
_____
_____
_____
_____
_____
_____
_____
_____
_____

I am grateful for _____

_____
_____
_____
_____
_____
_____
_____
_____
_____
_____
_____

Have a conversation with your inner goddess, what does she have to tell you?

Set your New Moon intentions:

Set your New Moon intentions:

New Moon

On this day _____

My intentions are _____

_____

_____

_____

_____

_____

_____

_____

_____

_____

I am grateful for _____

_____

_____

_____

_____

_____

_____

_____

_____

_____

_____

_____

On this day _____

My intentions are _____

I am grateful for _____

On this day

My intentions are

I am grateful for

On this day

My intentions are

I am grateful for

On this day

My intentions are

I am grateful for

On this day

My intentions are

I am grateful for

On this day _____

My intentions are _____

I am grateful for _____

On this day _____

My intentions are _____

_____
_____
_____
_____
_____
_____
_____
_____
_____

I am grateful for _____

_____
_____
_____
_____
_____
_____
_____
_____
_____

On this day

My intentions are

I am grateful for

On this day

My intentions are

I am grateful for

On this day

My intentions are

I am grateful for

On this day

My intentions are

I am grateful for

On this day

My intentions are

I am grateful for

On this day _____

My intentions are _____

_____
_____
_____
_____
_____
_____
_____
_____
_____
_____

I am grateful for _____

_____
_____
_____
_____
_____
_____
_____
_____
_____
_____
_____

On this day

My intentions are

I am grateful for

Full Moon

On this day _____

My intentions are _____

_____
_____
_____
_____
_____
_____
_____
_____
_____

I am grateful for _____

_____
_____
_____
_____
_____
_____
_____
_____
_____
_____

On this day _____

My intentions are _____

_____
_____
_____
_____
_____
_____
_____
_____
_____

I am grateful for _____

_____
_____
_____
_____
_____
_____
_____
_____
_____

On this day

My intentions are

I am grateful for

On this day ....

My intentions are ....

....

....

....

....

....

....

....

I am grateful for ....

....

....

....

....

....

....

....

....

....

On this day

My intentions are

I am grateful for

On this day _____

My intentions are _____

_____

_____

_____

_____

_____

_____

_____

_____

_____

_____

I am grateful for _____

_____

_____

_____

_____

_____

_____

_____

_____

_____

_____

On this day

My intentions are

I am grateful for

On this day _____

My intentions are _____
_____
_____
_____
_____
_____
_____
_____
_____
_____

I am grateful for _____
_____
_____
_____
_____
_____
_____
_____
_____
_____
_____
_____
_____

On this day

My intentions are

I am grateful for

On this day _____

My intentions are _____

_____

_____

_____

_____

_____

_____

_____

_____

_____

I am grateful for _____

_____

_____

_____

_____

_____

_____

_____

_____

_____

_____

On this day

My intentions are

I am grateful for

On this day _____

My intentions are _____
_____
_____
_____
_____
_____
_____
_____
_____
_____
_____

I am grateful for _____
_____
_____
_____
_____
_____
_____
_____
_____
_____
_____
_____

On this day

My intentions are

I am grateful for

On this day _____

My intentions are _____

_____

_____

_____

_____

_____

_____

_____

_____

_____

I am grateful for _____

_____

_____

_____

_____

_____

_____

_____

_____

_____

_____

On this day

My intentions are

I am grateful for

Visualize and describe your life three years from now:

_____

_____

_____

_____

_____

_____

_____

_____

_____

_____

_____

Set your New Moon intentions:

Set your New Moon intentions:

New Moon

On this day

My intentions are

I am grateful for

On this day

My intentions are

I am grateful for

On this day _____

My intentions are _____

_____

_____

_____

_____

_____

_____

_____

_____

I am grateful for _____

_____

_____

_____

_____

_____

_____

_____

_____

On this day

My intentions are

I am grateful for

On this day _____

My intentions are _____

_____

_____

_____

_____

_____

_____

_____

_____

I am grateful for _____

_____

_____

_____

_____

_____

_____

_____

_____

_____

On this day

My intentions are

I am grateful for

On this day _____

My intentions are _____

_____

_____

_____

_____

_____

_____

_____

_____

_____

I am grateful for _____

_____

_____

_____

_____

_____

_____

_____

_____

On this day

My intentions are

I am grateful for

On this day _____

My intentions are _____

_____
_____
_____
_____
_____
_____
_____
_____
_____

I am grateful for _____

_____
_____
_____
_____
_____
_____
_____
_____
_____

On this day

My intentions are

I am grateful for

On this day _____

My intentions are _____

I am grateful for

On this day

My intentions are

I am grateful for

On this day _____

My intentions are _____
_____
_____
_____
_____
_____
_____
_____
_____
_____

I am grateful for _____
_____
_____
_____
_____
_____
_____
_____
_____

On this day

My intentions are

I am grateful for

On this day

My intentions are

I am grateful for

Full Moon

On this day
_____

My intentions are
_____

_____

_____

_____

_____

_____

_____

_____

_____

I am grateful for
_____

_____

_____

_____

_____

_____

_____

_____

_____

_____

On this day

My intentions are

I am grateful for

On this day

My intentions are

I am grateful for

On this day _____

My intentions are _____

_____

_____

_____

_____

_____

_____

_____

_____

I am grateful for _____

_____

_____

_____

_____

_____

_____

_____

_____

_____

On this day

My intentions are

I am grateful for

On this day _____

My intentions are _____

_____

_____

_____

_____

_____

_____

_____

_____

I am grateful for _____

_____

_____

_____

_____

_____

_____

_____

_____

On this day _____

My intentions are _____

_____

_____

_____

_____

_____

_____

_____

_____

_____

I am grateful for _____

_____

_____

_____

_____

_____

_____

_____

_____

_____

_____

On this day _____

My intentions are _____

I am grateful for

On this day

My intentions are

I am grateful for

On this day _____

My intentions are _____

_____

_____

_____

_____

_____

_____

_____

_____

I am grateful for _____

_____

_____

_____

_____

_____

_____

On this day

My intentions are

I am grateful for

On this day

My intentions are

I am grateful for

On this day

My intentions are

I am grateful for

On this day _____

My intentions are _____

I am grateful for _____

On this day

My intentions are

I am grateful for

Write at least ten reasons why you are already living the life of your dreams:

_____

_____

_____

_____

_____

_____

_____

_____

_____

_____

_____

_____

"I'd Love To Hear From You!"

I know how much this Intentional Day Planner has impacted my life and it would be a pleasure to hear about how it's positively impacting yours as well. Please take a few moments and write down your story. Then go to the web link on the next page and submit the story for cosideration to be published in the next printing of this book.

Please submit your story/testimonial at the following web link:
www.IntentionalDayPlanner.com/mystory

Set your New Moon intentions:

Set your New Moon intentions:

New Moon

On this day _____

My intentions are

_____
_____
_____
_____
_____
_____
_____
_____
_____
_____

I am grateful for

_____
_____
_____
_____
_____
_____
_____
_____
_____
_____
_____

On this day

My intentions are

I am grateful for

On this day _____

My intentions are _____

I am grateful for _____

On this day _____

My intentions are _____

_____

_____

_____

_____

_____

_____

_____

_____

_____

_____

I am grateful for _____

_____

_____

_____

_____

_____

_____

_____

_____

_____

On this day _____

My intentions are

_____
_____
_____
_____
_____
_____
_____
_____
_____

I am grateful for

_____
_____
_____
_____
_____
_____
_____
_____
_____

On this day

My intentions are

I am grateful for

On this day

My intentions are

I am grateful for

On this day

My intentions are

I am grateful for

On this day _____

My intentions are _____

_____

_____

_____

_____

_____

_____

_____

_____

I am grateful for

_____

_____

_____

_____

_____

_____

_____

_____

_____

_____

On this day _____

My intentions are _____

_____

_____

_____

_____

_____

_____

_____

_____

_____

I am grateful for _____

_____

_____

_____

_____

_____

_____

_____

_____

_____

On this day _____

My intentions are _____

I am grateful for

On this day _____

My intentions are _____

_____

_____

_____

_____

_____

_____

_____

_____

_____

_____

I am grateful for _____

_____

_____

_____

_____

_____

_____

_____

_____

_____

_____

On this day _____

My intentions are _____

I am grateful for _____

On this day _____

My intentions are _____

_____

_____

_____

_____

_____

_____

_____

_____

_____

I am grateful for _____

_____

_____

_____

_____

_____

_____

_____

_____

_____

On this day

My intentions are

I am grateful for

Full Moon

On this day _____

My intentions are _____

_____

_____

_____

_____

_____

_____

_____

_____

_____

I am grateful for _____

_____

_____

_____

_____

_____

_____

_____

_____

On this day

My intentions are

I am grateful for

On this day _____

My intentions are _____
_____
_____
_____
_____
_____
_____
_____
_____
_____
_____
_____

I am grateful for _____
_____
_____
_____
_____
_____
_____
_____
_____
_____
_____
_____
_____

On this day

My intentions are

I am grateful for

On this day _____

My intentions are _____

_____

_____

_____

_____

_____

_____

_____

_____

_____

I am grateful for _____

_____

_____

_____

_____

_____

_____

_____

_____

On this day _____

My intentions are _____

I am grateful for

On this day _____

My intentions are _____

_____
_____
_____
_____
_____
_____
_____
_____
_____
_____

I am grateful for _____

_____
_____
_____
_____
_____
_____
_____
_____
_____
_____
_____
_____

On this day _____

My intentions are _____

I am grateful for _____

On this day _____

My intentions are _____

_____

_____

_____

_____

_____

_____

_____

_____

_____

I am grateful for _____

_____

_____

_____

_____

_____

_____

_____

_____

_____

_____

On this day _____

My intentions are _____

I am grateful for _____

On this day

My intentions are

I am grateful for

On this day _____

My intentions are _____
_____
_____
_____
_____
_____
_____
_____
_____
_____

I am grateful for _____
_____
_____
_____
_____
_____
_____
_____
_____
_____
_____

On this day _____

My intentions are _____

_____

_____

_____

_____

_____

_____

_____

_____

_____

I am grateful for _____

_____

_____

_____

_____

_____

_____

_____

_____

On this day

My intentions are

I am grateful for

On this day _____

My intentions are _____

_____
_____
_____
_____
_____
_____
_____
_____
_____
_____

I am grateful for _____

_____
_____
_____
_____
_____
_____
_____
_____
_____
_____

Write down all the miracles that you have witnessed in your life or the lives of others:

Set your New Moon intentions:

Set your New Moon intentions:

New Moon

On this day _____

My intentions are _____

_____
_____
_____
_____
_____
_____
_____
_____
_____

I am grateful for _____

_____
_____
_____
_____
_____
_____
_____
_____
_____

On this day _____

My intentions are _____

_____

_____

_____

_____

_____

_____

_____

_____

_____

I am grateful for _____

_____

_____

_____

_____

_____

_____

_____

_____

_____

_____

On this day

My intentions are

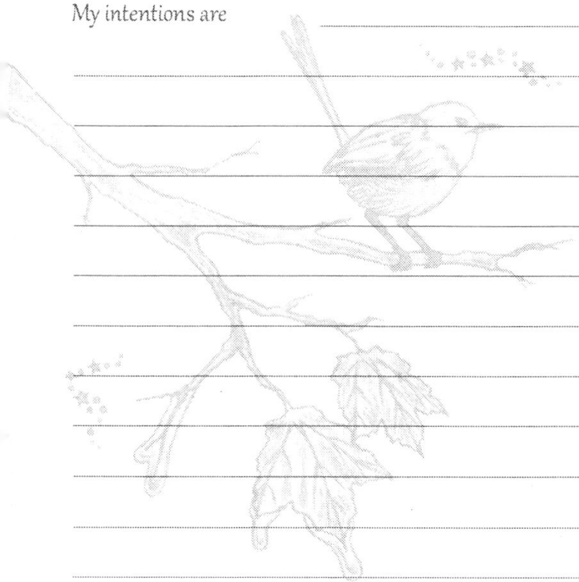

I am grateful for

On this day _____

My intentions are _____

_____

_____

_____

_____

_____

_____

_____

_____

_____

I am grateful for _____

_____

_____

_____

_____

_____

_____

_____

_____

_____

On this day _____

My intentions are _____

_____
_____
_____
_____
_____
_____
_____
_____
_____

I am grateful for _____

_____
_____
_____
_____
_____
_____
_____
_____
_____

On this day

My intentions are

I am grateful for

On this day _____

My intentions are _____

_____
_____
_____
_____
_____
_____
_____
_____
_____
_____
_____

I am grateful for _____

_____
_____
_____
_____
_____
_____
_____
_____
_____

On this day _____

My intentions are _____

_____
_____
_____
_____
_____
_____
_____
_____
_____
_____

I am grateful for _____

_____
_____
_____
_____
_____
_____
_____
_____
_____
_____
_____
_____
_____

On this day _____

My intentions are _____

_____

_____

_____

_____

_____

_____

_____

_____

_____

I am grateful for _____

_____

_____

_____

_____

_____

_____

_____

_____

On this day _____

My intentions are _____

_____

_____

_____

_____

_____

_____

_____

_____

_____

I am grateful for _____

_____

_____

_____

_____

_____

_____

_____

_____

_____

_____

On this day

My intentions are

I am grateful for

On this day _____

My intentions are _____

_____

_____

_____

_____

_____

_____

_____

_____

_____

_____

I am grateful for _____

_____

_____

_____

_____

_____

_____

_____

_____

_____

_____

On this day

My intentions are

I am grateful for

On this day _____

My intentions are _____

_____
_____
_____
_____
_____
_____
_____
_____
_____

I am grateful for _____

_____
_____
_____
_____
_____
_____
_____
_____
_____
_____
_____
_____

On this day _____

My intentions are _____

I am grateful for _____

Full Moon   On this day _____

My intentions are _____

_____

_____

_____

_____

_____

_____

_____

_____

_____

_____

I am grateful for _____

_____

_____

_____

_____

_____

_____

_____

_____

_____

_____

_____

On this day _____

My intentions are _____

I am grateful for _____

On this day _____

My intentions are _____

_____

_____

_____

_____

_____

_____

_____

_____

_____

_____

I am grateful for _____

_____

_____

_____

_____

_____

_____

_____

_____

_____

_____

On this day _____

My intentions are _____

_____

_____

_____

_____

_____

_____

_____

_____

_____

I am grateful for _____

_____

_____

_____

_____

_____

_____

_____

_____

On this day _____

My intentions are _____

_____
_____
_____
_____
_____
_____
_____
_____
_____
_____

I am grateful for _____

_____
_____
_____
_____
_____
_____
_____
_____
_____
_____
_____
_____

On this day _____

My intentions are _____
_____
_____
_____
_____
_____
_____
_____
_____
_____

I am grateful for _____
_____
_____
_____
_____
_____
_____
_____
_____

On this day _____

My intentions are _____

_____

_____

_____

_____

_____

_____

_____

_____

_____

I am grateful for _____

_____

_____

_____

_____

_____

_____

_____

_____

_____

_____

On this day _____

My intentions are _____

I am grateful for _____

On this day

My intentions are

_____

_____

_____

_____

_____

_____

_____

_____

_____

I am grateful for

_____

_____

_____

_____

_____

_____

_____

_____

_____

_____

_____

On this day

My intentions are

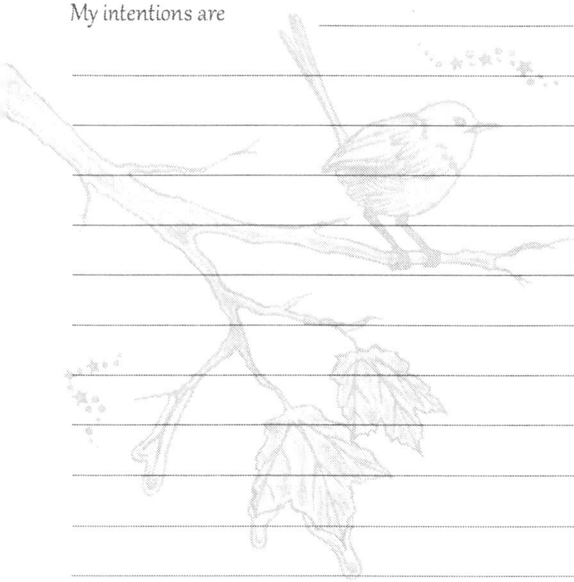

I am grateful for

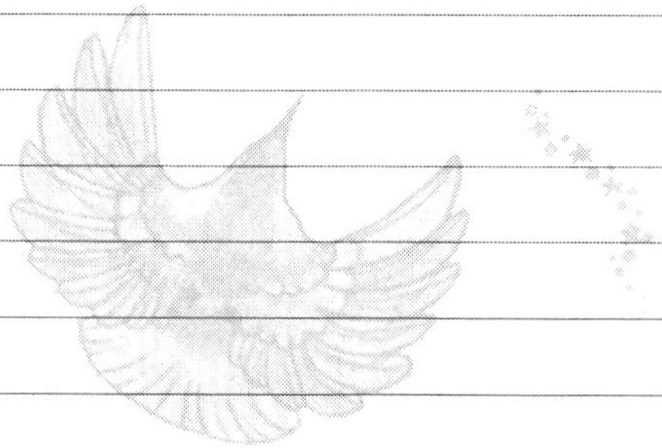

On this day _____

My intentions are _____

_____

_____

_____

_____

_____

_____

_____

_____

I am grateful for _____

_____

_____

_____

_____

_____

_____

_____

_____

On this day

My intentions are

I am grateful for

On this day _____

My intentions are _____

_____
_____
_____
_____
_____
_____
_____
_____
_____

I am grateful for _____

_____
_____
_____
_____
_____
_____
_____
_____
_____
_____
_____
_____

On this day _____

My intentions are _____

_____
_____
_____
_____
_____
_____
_____
_____
_____
_____

I am grateful for _____

_____
_____
_____
_____
_____
_____
_____
_____
_____

On this day _____

My intentions are _____

_____

_____

_____

_____

_____

_____

_____

_____

I am grateful for _____

_____

_____

_____

_____

_____

_____

_____

_____

Tell me ten ways you could anchor more joy into your everyday experience.

Set your New Moon intentions:

Set your New Moon intentions:

New Moon　　On this day

My intentions are

I am grateful for

On this day _____

My intentions are _____

_____

_____

_____

_____

_____

_____

_____

_____

_____

_____

I am grateful for _____

_____

_____

_____

_____

_____

_____

_____

_____

_____

_____

_____

_____

_____

On this day

My intentions are

I am grateful for

On this day

My intentions are

I am grateful for

On this day

My intentions are

I am grateful for

On this day

My intentions are

I am grateful for

On this day _____

My intentions are _____

I am grateful for _____

On this day

My intentions are

I am grateful for

On this day

My intentions are

I am grateful for

On this day ....

My intentions are ....

_____

_____

_____

_____

_____

_____

_____

_____

_____

I am grateful for ....

_____

_____

_____

_____

_____

_____

_____

_____

_____

_____

On this day _____

My intentions are _____

_____

_____

_____

_____

_____

_____

_____

_____

I am grateful for _____

_____

_____

_____

_____

_____

_____

_____

On this day _____

My intentions are

_____

_____

_____

_____

_____

_____

_____

_____

_____

_____

I am grateful for

_____

_____

_____

_____

_____

_____

_____

_____

_____

_____

_____

_____

On this day _____

My intentions are _____

I am grateful for _____

On this day _____

My intentions are _____

_____

_____

_____

_____

_____

_____

_____

_____

_____

I am grateful for _____

_____

_____

_____

_____

_____

_____

_____

_____

_____

_____

_____

On this day

My intentions are

I am grateful for

Full Moon

On this day

My intentions are

I am grateful for

On this day _____

My intentions are _____

_____

_____

_____

_____

_____

_____

_____

I am grateful for _____

_____

_____

_____

_____

_____

_____

_____

_____

On this day

My intentions are

I am grateful for

On this day ....

My intentions are ....

I am grateful for ....

On this day ....

My intentions are ....

....

....

....

....

....

....

....

....

I am grateful for ....

....

....

....

....

....

....

....

....

....

....

....

On this day

My intentions are

I am grateful for

On this day

My intentions are

I am grateful for

On this day _____

My intentions are _____

_____

_____

_____

_____

_____

_____

I am grateful for _____

_____

_____

_____

_____

_____

_____

On this day

My intentions are

I am grateful for

On this day

My intentions are

I am grateful for

On this day

My intentions are

I am grateful for

On this day

My intentions are

I am grateful for

On this day

My intentions are

I am grateful for

On this day

My intentions are

I am grateful for

On this day

My intentions are

I am grateful for

What do you believe about yourself? about life?

_____

_____

_____

_____

_____

_____

_____

_____

_____

_____

_____

Set your New Moon intentions:

Set your New Moon intentions:

New Moon

On this day _____

My intentions are _____

_____

_____

_____

_____

_____

_____

_____

_____

I am grateful for _____

_____

_____

_____

_____

_____

_____

_____

_____

On this day

My intentions are

I am grateful for

On this day _____

My intentions are _____

_____

_____

_____

_____

_____

_____

_____

_____

_____

I am grateful for _____

_____

_____

_____

_____

_____

_____

_____

_____

On this day _____

My intentions are _____

_____

_____

_____

_____

_____

_____

_____

_____

_____

I am grateful for _____

_____

_____

_____

_____

_____

_____

_____

_____

_____

_____

_____

On this day

My intentions are

I am grateful for

On this day

My intentions are

I am grateful for

On this day _____

My intentions are
_____
_____
_____
_____
_____
_____
_____
_____
_____
_____

I am grateful for
_____
_____
_____
_____
_____
_____
_____
_____
_____
_____

On this day _____

My intentions are _____

_____

_____

_____

_____

_____

_____

_____

_____

I am grateful for _____

_____

_____

_____

_____

_____

_____

_____

_____

_____

_____

On this day

My intentions are

I am grateful for

On this day _____

My intentions are _____

_____

_____

_____

_____

_____

_____

_____

I am grateful for _____

_____

_____

_____

_____

_____

_____

_____

_____

_____

On this day _____

My intentions are _____

_____

_____

_____

_____

_____

_____

_____

_____

_____

_____

I am grateful for _____

_____

_____

_____

_____

_____

_____

_____

_____

_____

www.IntentionalDayPlanner.com

On this day

My intentions are

I am grateful for

On this day

My intentions are

I am grateful for

On this day _____

My intentions are _____

_____

_____

_____

_____

_____

_____

_____

_____

I am grateful for _____

_____

_____

_____

_____

_____

_____

_____

_____

_____

_____

On this day _____

My intentions are _____

_____

_____

_____

_____

_____

_____

_____

_____

I am grateful for _____

_____

_____

_____

_____

_____

_____

_____

_____

Full Moon

On this day

My intentions are

I am grateful for

On this day

My intentions are

I am grateful for

On this day

My intentions are

I am grateful for

On this day _____

My intentions are _____
_____
_____
_____
_____
_____
_____
_____
_____
_____
_____

I am grateful for _____
_____
_____
_____
_____
_____
_____
_____
_____
_____
_____

On this day _____

My intentions are _____

_____

_____

_____

_____

_____

_____

_____

_____

_____

I am grateful for _____

_____

_____

_____

_____

_____

_____

_____

_____

_____

_____

_____

_____

On this day

My intentions are

I am grateful for

On this day ....

My intentions are ....

....

....

....

....

....

....

....

....

I am grateful for ....

....

....

....

....

....

....

....

....

....

....

On this day

My intentions are

_____

_____

_____

_____

_____

_____

_____

_____

I am grateful for

_____

_____

_____

_____

_____

_____

_____

On this day

_____

My intentions are

_____

_____

_____

_____

_____

_____

_____

_____

_____

_____

I am grateful for

_____

_____

_____

_____

_____

_____

_____

_____

_____

_____

_____

_____

On this day

My intentions are

I am grateful for

On this day _____

My intentions are _____

_____

_____

_____

_____

_____

_____

_____

I am grateful for _____

_____

_____

_____

_____

_____

_____

_____

_____

_____

_____

On this day

My intentions are

I am grateful for

On this day

My intentions are

_____

_____

_____

_____

_____

_____

_____

_____

_____

I am grateful for

_____

_____

_____

_____

_____

_____

_____

_____

_____

_____

_____

On this day

My intentions are

I am grateful for

On this day _____

My intentions are _____

_____

_____

_____

_____

_____

_____

I am grateful for _____

_____

_____

_____

_____

_____

_____

_____

_____

What do you need to clear out of your life?
What would you like to change?

Set your New Moon intentions:

Set your New Moon intentions:

New Moon

On this day

My intentions are

I am grateful for

On this day _____

My intentions are _____

_____

_____

_____

_____

_____

_____

_____

_____

I am grateful for _____

_____

_____

_____

_____

_____

_____

_____

_____

_____

On this day ....

My intentions are ....

....

....

....

....

....

....

....

....

I am grateful for ....

....

....

....

....

....

....

....

On this day _____

My intentions are _____

_____

_____

_____

_____

_____

_____

_____

_____

_____

I am grateful for _____

_____

_____

_____

_____

_____

_____

_____

_____

On this day _____

My intentions are _____

I am grateful for

On this day

My intentions are

I am grateful for

On this day _____

My intentions are _____

_____

_____

_____

_____

_____

_____

_____

_____

_____

I am grateful for _____

_____

_____

_____

_____

_____

_____

_____

On this day _____

My intentions are _____

_____

_____

_____

_____

_____

_____

_____

I am grateful for _____

_____

_____

_____

_____

_____

_____

On this day _____

My intentions are _____

_____

_____

_____

_____

_____

_____

_____

_____

_____

I am grateful for _____

_____

_____

_____

_____

_____

_____

On this day

My intentions are

I am grateful for

On this day _____

My intentions are _____

I am grateful for _____

On this day _____

My intentions are _____

_____

_____

_____

_____

_____

_____

_____

I am grateful for _____

_____

_____

_____

_____

_____

_____

_____

On this day

My intentions are

I am grateful for

On this day

My intentions are

I am grateful for

On this day

My intentions are

I am grateful for

Full Moon

On this day _____

My intentions are _____

_____

_____

_____

_____

_____

_____

I am grateful for _____

_____

_____

_____

_____

_____

_____

On this day

My intentions are

I am grateful for

On this day

My intentions are

I am grateful for

On this day _____

My intentions are _____

_____

_____

_____

_____

_____

_____

_____

_____

_____

I am grateful for _____

_____

_____

_____

_____

_____

_____

_____

On this day

My intentions are

I am grateful for

On this day _____

My intentions are _____

_____

_____

_____

_____

_____

_____

_____

_____

_____

I am grateful for _____

_____

_____

_____

_____

_____

_____

_____

On this day

My intentions are

I am grateful for

On this day   _____

My intentions are   _____

_____

_____

_____

_____

_____

_____

_____

_____

_____

I am grateful for   _____

_____

_____

_____

_____

_____

_____

_____

_____

On this day

My intentions are

I am grateful for

On this day ....

My intentions are ....

....

....

....

....

....

....

....

....

I am grateful for ....

....

....

....

....

....

....

On this day _____

My intentions are _____

_____

_____

_____

_____

_____

_____

_____

_____

I am grateful for _____

_____

_____

_____

_____

_____

_____

_____

_____

_____

On this day

My intentions are

I am grateful for

On this day _____

My intentions are _____

_____

_____

_____

_____

_____

_____

_____

_____

I am grateful for _____

_____

_____

_____

_____

_____

_____

_____

_____

On this day _____

My intentions are _____

_____

_____

_____

_____

_____

_____

_____

I am grateful for _____

_____

_____

_____

_____

_____

_____

_____

_____

_____

On this day

My intentions are

I am grateful for

What do you need to make more room for in your life?

Get Ready For The Next 13 Moon Cycles Pre-Order Now!

As you head into your 12th moon calendar, we can only assume that you are enjoying your Intentional Day Planner and we would like to remind you to order your next copy right away so that you can keep the momentum going strong.

We've made it simple for you to re-order, simply visit our website link below and you can get your copy delivered before you run out of pages in this copy. www.IntentionalDayPlanner.com/reorder

Here's a short story of two Intentional Day Planner users:

Two ladies browsed upon an interesting website one day. They both felt as if the content spoke directly to their current life challenges. Wanting to have a place where they could express, explore and grow like they've never done before.

They both found themselves excited to click through the ordering process and anxiously await their copy in the mail.

A few days later a package arrived and the paper wrapping couldn't have been ripped off fast enough to unveil a fresh copy of their first Intentional Day Planner.

Even though they were excited to get started, they had no idea the impact such a simple, yet profound, practice would have on thier lives.

Slowly but surely the pages began to fill up more and more as the weeks and months passed by. Things were changing... improving... evolving into one amazing day after another.

www.IntentionalDayPlanner.com

Then they began the 12th moon cycle, BUT one lady forgot to order her next copy and as the 13th month passed by there were signs of the joy, happiness and freedom slowing down.

The lady who ordered her new copy didn't miss a beat and began her next 13 moon cycles with clearly defined intentions for the following year.

The lady who forgot found that, because there wasn't immediate and easy access to the Intentional Day Planner, she felt something missing from her day and before too long "LIFE" filled in that gap with other less fulfilling tasks, activities and obligations.

It was hard to stay anchored in her heart without her daily commitments and tools to keep her on track. That expression, exploration and growth began to rapidly decline and memories of the stresses, anxieties and disappointments from the past crept back into their comfortable homes.

The lady who was proactive and ordered, went on to enjoy many years of Intentional Day Planners and actively took part in creating her greatest adventures one day at a time.

**Don't Miss Out
On The Next 13 Months Of
Actively Creating
Your Greatest Adventure!**

What the Intentional Day Planner Will Do For You:

Gives you a place for your creative expression.

Allows you to explore more of who you really are.

Stores valuable memories, ideas and inspirations.

Keeps you in sync and in alignment with the lunar cycles.

*Simply go to our website with the following link:
www.IntentionalDayPlanner.com/reorder*

Set your New Moon intentions:

Set your New Moon intentions:

New Moon

On this day _____

My intentions are _____

_____

_____

_____

_____

_____

_____

_____

_____

I am grateful for _____

_____

_____

_____

_____

_____

_____

_____

_____

_____

_____

_____

On this day

My intentions are

I am grateful for

On this day

My intentions are

I am grateful for

On this day

My intentions are

I am grateful for

On this day _____

My intentions are _____
_____
_____
_____
_____

_____
_____
_____

I am grateful for _____
_____
_____
_____
_____
_____
_____
_____
_____

On this day

My intentions are

I am grateful for

On this day

My intentions are

I am grateful for

On this day _____

My intentions are

_____

_____

_____

_____

_____

_____

_____

_____

_____

_____

I am grateful for

_____

_____

_____

_____

_____

_____

_____

_____

_____

On this day

My intentions are

I am grateful for

On this day _____

My intentions are _____

_____

_____

_____

_____

_____

_____

_____

_____

_____

I am grateful for _____

_____

_____

_____

_____

_____

_____

_____

_____

On this day

My intentions are

I am grateful for

On this day

My intentions are

I am grateful for

On this day

My intentions are

I am grateful for

On this day

My intentions are

I am grateful for

On this day

My intentions are

I am grateful for

Full Moon

On this day

My intentions are

I am grateful for

On this day

My intentions are

I am grateful for

On this day

My intentions are

I am grateful for

On this day

My intentions are

I am grateful for

On this day

My intentions are

I am grateful for

On this day _____

My intentions are
_____
_____
_____
_____
_____
_____

_____
_____
_____
_____

I am grateful for
_____
_____
_____
_____
_____
_____
_____
_____
_____
_____

On this day _____

My intentions are _____

_____

_____

_____

_____

_____

_____

_____

_____

I am grateful for _____

_____

_____

_____

_____

_____

_____

_____

On this day

My intentions are

I am grateful for

On this day

My intentions are

I am grateful for

On this day _____

My intentions are _____

_____

_____

_____

_____

_____

_____

_____

_____

I am grateful for _____

_____

_____

_____

_____

_____

_____

_____

_____

_____

On this day

My intentions are

I am grateful for

On this day _____

My intentions are _____

_____

_____

_____

_____

_____

_____

_____

_____

_____

I am grateful for _____

_____

_____

_____

_____

_____

_____

_____

_____

_____

_____

On this day _____

My intentions are _____

_____

_____

_____

_____

_____

_____

_____

I am grateful for _____

_____

_____

_____

_____

_____

_____

_____

_____

On this day _____

My intentions are _____

_____

_____

_____

_____

_____

_____

_____

_____

_____

I am grateful for _____

_____

_____

_____

_____

_____

_____

_____

_____

_____

On this day

My intentions are

I am grateful for

What else is possible in your life at this moment?

Set your New Moon intentions:

Set your New Moon intentions:

New Moon

On this day

My intentions are

I am grateful for

On this day

My intentions are

I am grateful for

On this day _____

My intentions are _____

I am grateful for

On this day _____

My intentions are _____

_____

_____

_____

_____

_____

_____

_____

_____

I am grateful for _____

_____

_____

_____

_____

_____

_____

_____

_____

On this day

My intentions are

I am grateful for

On this day _____

My intentions are _____

_____

_____

_____

_____

_____

_____

_____

_____

_____

I am grateful for _____

_____

_____

_____

_____

_____

_____

_____

_____

_____

On this day _____

My intentions are _____

I am grateful for

On this day _____

My intentions are _____

_____

_____

_____

_____

_____

_____

_____

_____

_____

I am grateful for _____

_____

_____

_____

_____

_____

_____

_____

_____

On this day

My intentions are

I am grateful for

On this day _____

My intentions are _____

_____
_____
_____
_____
_____
_____
_____
_____
_____
_____

I am grateful for _____

_____
_____
_____
_____
_____
_____
_____
_____
_____
_____

On this day _____

My intentions are _____

_____
_____
_____
_____
_____
_____
_____
_____
_____
_____

I am grateful for
_____
_____
_____
_____
_____
_____
_____
_____
_____
_____
_____
_____

On this day _____

My intentions are _____

_____
_____
_____
_____
_____
_____
_____
_____
_____

I am grateful for _____

_____
_____
_____
_____
_____
_____
_____
_____
_____

On this day _____

My intentions are _____

_____
_____
_____
_____
_____
_____
_____
_____
_____

I am grateful for
_____
_____
_____
_____
_____
_____
_____
_____
_____
_____
_____
_____

On this day

My intentions are

I am grateful for

On this day _____

My intentions are _____

_____

_____

_____

_____

_____

_____

_____

_____

I am grateful for _____

_____

_____

_____

_____

_____

_____

_____

_____

_____

_____

Full Moon

On this day _____

My intentions are _____

_____

_____

_____

_____

_____

_____

_____

_____

_____

I am grateful for _____

_____

_____

_____

_____

_____

_____

_____

_____

_____

_____

On this day _____

My intentions are _____

I am grateful for

On this day _____

My intentions are _____

_____

_____

_____

_____

_____

_____

_____

_____

I am grateful for _____

_____

_____

_____

_____

_____

_____

_____

_____

On this day _____

My intentions are _____

_____

_____

_____

_____

_____

_____

_____

I am grateful for _____

_____

_____

_____

_____

_____

_____

On this day _____

My intentions are _____

_____

_____

_____

_____

_____

_____

_____

_____

I am grateful for _____

_____

_____

_____

_____

_____

_____

_____

_____

_____

On this day _____

My intentions are _____

I am grateful for

On this day _____

My intentions are _____

_____

_____

_____

_____

_____

_____

_____

_____

_____

I am grateful for _____

_____

_____

_____

_____

_____

_____

_____

_____

_____

_____

On this day _____

My intentions are _____

_____

_____

_____

_____

_____

_____

_____

_____

I am grateful for _____

_____

_____

_____

_____

_____

_____

_____

_____

On this day _____

My intentions are _____

_____

_____

_____

_____

_____

_____

_____

_____

_____

I am grateful for _____

_____

_____

_____

_____

_____

_____

_____

_____

On this day _____

My intentions are _____

_____

_____

_____

_____

_____

_____

_____

_____

_____

I am grateful for _____

_____

_____

_____

_____

_____

_____

_____

_____

On this day

My intentions are

I am grateful for

On this day _____

My intentions are _____

_____

_____

_____

_____

_____

_____

_____

_____

I am grateful for _____

_____

_____

_____

_____

_____

_____

_____

_____

On this day _____

My intentions are _____

_____

_____

_____

_____

_____

_____

_____

_____

_____

I am grateful for _____

_____

_____

_____

_____

_____

_____

_____

_____

On this day _____

My intentions are _____

_____

_____

_____

_____

_____

_____

_____

I am grateful for _____

_____

_____

_____

_____

_____

_____

On this day _____

My intentions are _____

I am grateful for _____

Write down ten things you are saying YES to and ten actions you are going to take to make thing happen!

Get Ready For The Next 13 Moon Cycles Pre-Order Now!

You still have time to order your next copy of your Intentional Day Planner. Take a few moments and flip through this planner and notice all the amazing things that you've been able to accomplish and all you were grateful for through the last 13 moon cycles.

Now it's time to continue that momentum and stay in sync with the lunar cycles as you maintain an active role in creating a life you desire.

We've made it simple for you to re-order, simply visit our website link below and you can get your new Intentional Day Planner delivered before you run out of pages in this copy.
www.IntentionalDayPlanner.com/reorder

Here's a continuation of the short story:

The lady who pre-ordered, just kept her stride strong and enjoyed the uninterupted flow of creating her intentions, contemplating deep questions and taking progressive action towards her inner fulfilment and joy.

The other lady realized that she was so wrapped up in the amazing life that was unfolding day after day that she somehow forgot to order her Intentional Day Planner and immediately went to the web link suggested to place the order.

A few days passed and she used it as time for reflection and connecting with her heart to realign with her deepest desires and treasured memories.

When the book arrived she tore open the wrapping like an over excited child on Christmas morning. Once again she felt on track with where she was headed and made a mental note to pre-order next time to eliminate any interruption in her daily intentions and gratitudes.

Both ladies, came to realize that the daily practice was now a fully integrated habit that they couldn't live without. In fact they began to think about other women in their circles whom they could send the Intentional Day Planner to as a gift.

List 3 women you think would benefit from using an Intentional Day Planner and consider adding a copy for them to your order:

_____

_____

Don't Miss Out
On The Next 13 Months Of
Actively Creating
Your Greatest Adventure!

What the Intentional Day Planner Will Do For You:
Gives you a place for your creative expression.
Allows you to explore more of who you really are.
Stores valuable memories, ideas and inspirations.
Keeps you in sync and in alignment with the lunar cycles.

Simply go to our website with the following link:
www.IntentionalDayPlanner.com/reorder

Thank you for using The Intentional Day Planner,
and if you would like to continue co-creating your reality and
realizing your dreams, visit intentionaldayplanner.com to join
our community and order another Intentional Day planner.

May the magic of this life
always fill you with joy and wonder!

Intentional Day Planner Publication.

43613324R00277

Made in the USA
Charleston, SC
30 June 2015